Date Due

JUN 0 1 2015			

The First Solo Flight Around the World

**The Story of Wiley Post and His Airplane,
the Winnie Mae**

The First Solo Flight Around the World

**The Story of Wiley Post and His Airplane,
the Winnie Mae**

by Richard L. Taylor

Franklin Watts
New York / London / Toronto / Sydney
A First Book

Photographs copyright ©: Cover: UPI/Bettmann and Tony Stone Worldwide; 6, 39: Lockheed-California Company; 10 (top), 10–11 (spread): EEA Aviation Foundation, Boeing Aeronautical Library; 10 (bottom), 13, 17, 18, 31, 44–45, 45, 53, 54, 54–55, 57 (bottom), 60: UPI/Bettmann; 23, 27, 30–31, 33, 34–35, 35, 43, 47, 50–51, 51, 56: Oklahoma Historical Society; 38, 58: NASM, Smithsonian Institution; 57 (top and middle): AP/Wide World

Library of Congress Cataloging-in-Publication Data
Taylor, Richard L.
The first solo flight around the world: the story of Wiley Post and his airplane,
the Winnie Mae / by Richard L. Taylor.
p. cm. — (A First book)
Includes bibliographical references (p.) and index.
Summary: Covers the life of American pilot Wiley Post and his record-setting solo flight
around the world in 1933.
ISBN 0-531-20160-0 (lib. bdg.)
1. Post, Wiley, 1898–1935—Juvenile literature. 2. Air Pilots—United States—
Biography—Juvenile literature. 3. Flights around the world—Juvenile literature.
4. Winnie Mae (Airplane)—Juvenile literature. [1. Post, Wiley, 1898–1935. 2. Air pilots.
3. Flights around the world. 4. Winnie Mae (Airplane)] I. Title. II. Series.
TL540.P65T38 1993
629.13'092—dc20   93-6880
[B]   CIP
         AC
         Rev.

Contents

THE **WINNIE MA**
OF OKLAHOMA

LOS ANGELES TO CHICAGO · 9 HRS. 9 MIN. 4 SEC. · AUG. 2?
AROUND THE WORLD · 8 DAYS, 15 HRS. 51 MIN. · JUNE 23 TO
AROUND THE WORLD · 7 DAYS, 18 HRS. 49 MIN. · JULY 15 TO JU

Frontiers to Conquer

The 1930s were golden years for aviation in the United States. Instead of barely noticing airplanes as we do today, people stopped what they were doing when a plane flew overhead and watched until it was out of sight. Pilots were considered supermen, and most of them were engaged in a constant race to see who could go faster, fly higher, and travel farther. The intense interest in flying created a lot of invention and development in the 1930s. Airplane builders sprang up all over the country. Many of them failed, but some of them produced flying machines that broke records almost as fast as they were set.

Record-breaking performances also meant that the frontiers of aviation were being conquered. Large bodies of water — the Atlantic and Pacific Oceans, for example — had been crossed by aircraft. Pilots had flown across the major continents of the world and had reached speeds that were truly remarkable for the time.

Today, the sound barrier has been broken, pilots have flown around the world without stopping, and airplanes have climbed to the upper limits of the atmosphere. There are few (if any) frontiers remaining. But in 1933, no one had flown all the way around the world all alone; this was one of the last "firsts" in aviation.

Wiley Hardeman Post took up the challenge and departed from Floyd Bennett Field in New York City on July 15, 1933. Seven days later, he landed at the same airfield after circling the globe and became the first person to fly around the world by himself.

The Pilot

Until 1913, Wiley Post's life had been very ordinary, very difficult, and very dull.

Until 1913, when he was fifteen years old, Wiley Post had moved with his family from one poor farm to another in Texas and Oklahoma, working hard and getting nowhere.

Until 1913, Wiley Post had no idea what the future held for him. He had become so unhappy with school that he quit after finishing the eighth grade, and it looked like he would spend the rest of his life trying to earn a living from the soil. The only bright spot in his existence was his love of machinery — and living on a poor farm, he had plenty of opportunities to fix broken equipment.

But in 1913, Wiley Post went to the Oklahoma state fair, and his life was changed forever.

Not quite ten years after the Wright brothers had accomplished the world's first powered flight, stunt fly-

ing had become very popular at public gatherings in the United States. An aerobatic exhibition was one of the featured acts at the 1913 Oklahoma fair, and Post was entranced as he watched the pilot and airplane perform.

The course for Wiley Post's life was set. He knew that his future would be in flying; he had to become a pilot.

Unfortunately, lack of money and the First World War got in the way, and it would be thirteen years before Post earned his wings.

Stunt-flying exhibitions for the public were exceptionally popular in the early days of flying. Wing walking was always a crowd pleaser. (bottom left) **Wiley Post, age 5, and his younger sister Mary.**

During that time he entered a school for automobile mechanics, but couldn't afford to continue the classes and had to go back to the family farm. A short time later the war broke out, and Post joined the army, intending to become a radio operator. The war ended before the course was finished, however, and Wiley was once again a civilian without a job.

Drilling for oil was big business in Oklahoma in 1918, and Post got a high-paying job as a "roughneck" (the slang name for an oil-field laborer), but his thoughts were still in the sky. He took his first airplane ride that summer, and the pilot went through every aerobatic maneuver he knew. But as much as he wanted to become a pilot himself, there wasn't enough money to begin the training. Wiley kept working.

In 1924, an aerial exhibition once again changed Post's life. A flying circus called "Texas Topnotch Fliers" came to Wewoka, Oklahoma, and when Wiley found out that their regular parachutist had been injured, he offered to take his place.

There was no requirement for training in those early days of aviation, and Post soon found himself 2,000 feet (610 m) in the air, standing on the wing of an airplane with a parachute strapped on his back. His first parachute jump was one of the biggest thrills of his life, but more important, it got him started on his way to becoming a pilot. Wiley Post left the oil fields, became a member of the "Texas Topnotch Fliers," and jumped ninety-nine times in the next two years.

The air-circus pilots gave Post flying lessons from time to time as they traveled around the country, and in 1926, he made his first solo flight — a major milestone in every pilot's training. In 1926 pilots didn't need licenses; a person could buy an airplane and fly it to his heart's content. And that's just what Wiley Post intended to do.

Roughnecks made a lot more money than parachute jumpers, so Post quit the flying circus and went back to work in the oil fields. He intended to buy an airplane as soon as he could and get started on his career in aviation.

While Post was working on an oil rig, however, a steel chip flew from another roughneck's hammer and lodged in Wiley's left eye. The infection that followed could not be controlled, and the doctors had to remove the eye.

This would have been a serious problem for anyone, but it was even worse for a young man who wanted to become a pilot.

The loss of an eye means the loss of depth perception. We normally see things from a slightly different angle with each eye, and the difference in images lets us determine how far away things are. But with just one eye it becomes very difficult to judge distances — something that is very important for airplane pilots.

Wiley Post was a determined young man and decided he could overcome this problem. During the recovery from his surgery, he practiced by estimating the distance to a nearby tree or a house, then checked his accuracy by pacing off the distance. He trained himself so well that his depth perception eventually became almost as good as if he had both eyes.

Fully recovered, Post used the insurance payment from his accident to buy a secondhand airplane. He became a "barnstormer," traveling from town to town, taking people for rides, and giving flying lessons. All went well until the airplane was wrecked in an accident, and Post didn't have enough money to get it fixed. Once more, he was out of a job, but good luck was just around the corner.

At this time, late 1927, the oil business was still booming in the southwestern part of the United States, and whenever a new field was opened, the people who got there first were able to lease the best property. Fast transportation was very important. While searching for a job, Post happened to meet two oil-field developers who recognized that an airplane could get them to new sites ahead of their competitors. They bought a brand-new airplane — a three-seat Travel Air — and hired Post as their pilot.

Only one thing now stood between Wiley and his objective. The Aviation Act of 1926 required that all pilots have licenses issued by the government, and Post had to prove that he could fly safely with only one eye. He passed all the written examinations and flying tests, and was awarded a pilot certificate in September 1928. With a steady job, a good airplane, and filled with confidence in what he could do, Wiley Post was off and running.

The Lockheed Vega

The Loughhead brothers, airplane builders who had settled in California, changed the spelling of their last name to Lockheed and changed the aviation world's thinking about airplane design with their very first model — the Vega. (To this day, Lockheed airplanes are named after stars and constellations.)

The standard way to build an airplane in 1927 was to glue and nail and wire together a framework of wood, then cover it with fabric to reduce air resistance. Builders were limited by the materials and construction techniques available to them, which meant that most airplanes had flat surfaces and were not very streamlined.

Wings were built the same way; a series of ribs was fastened to a long wooden spar that ran from wingtip to wingtip. The size of a wing — and therefore the weight it could lift — was limited by the strength of the spar, and so most airplanes in the late 1920s were biplanes.

Allen Lockheed (center) and his brothers forever changed the direction of aviation history with the development of the Vega aircraft.

Wiley Post checks out aviation charts in preparation for a flight in the *Winnie Mae.*

They needed two wings, one mounted above the other, to develop enough lift for flight.

The Lockheed brothers changed all that when they built the first Vega. Instead of using straight pieces of wood to form a flat-sided, fabric-covered fuselage body, they made two rounded half-shells of spruce plywood, then glued them together. The resulting circular shape was very strong, much like an eggshell.

Vega wings were made of wooden ribs cut to the proper shape, but thin sheets of plywood were used instead of a fabric covering. In addition to producing a smooth surface, the plywood skin made the wing so much stronger that only one wing was needed. The Vega was a monoplane, with its single wing mounted on top of the fuselage. It was considerably stronger and lighter than other airplanes the same size.

There was room in the cabin for six passengers, and the pilot sat in a completely enclosed compartment between the leading edge of the wing and the engine. Although it was very small, the cockpit protected the pilot of a Vega from the wind, rain, and cold. The days of uncomfortable open cockpits were coming to an end.

The Vega's engine was also quite different from those on most other airplanes built in 1927. It was an air-cooled radial engine with seven cylinders arranged like the spokes of a wheel around a central crankshaft instead of being lined up in a row behind the propeller. And instead of a complicated and heavy water-cooling system, excess heat was carried away by the flow of air around each cylinder. The radial engine became very popular with airplane designers, because it could develop a great deal of power for each pound of engine weight.

As a final touch, the Vega was fitted with "wheel pants," streamlined covers that greatly reduced the drag of the landing gear. The combination of low weight, high power, and streamlining produced an airplane that out flew its competitors. The Vega's top speed was 135 miles (217 km) per hour, which was considered fast for a six-passenger airplane in 1927.

Soon after the Vega was introduced, Wiley Post's employers bought a brand new Vega and sent him to the Lockheed plant in California to take delivery. The new airplane was christened the *Winnie Mae,* after one of the oilmen's daughters.

Post flew only a few trips in the new Vega before the stock market crashed in 1929 and the Great Depression began. The oil business was hard hit, and the *Winnie Mae* had to go — and along with it, Post's job. When he returned the airplane to the plant he asked Lockheed for a job and was hired as a pilot and salesman.

During the next few months, Post made a number of test flights, delivered new airplanes to customers all around the country, and even flew Vegas for a short time as an airline pilot in Texas and Mexico. He became very familiar with this remarkable airplane and its capabilities. His in-depth knowledge of the Vega would prove extremely valuable on his long-distance flights.

The Winnie Mae Sets Her First Record

By June 1930, the oil business had recovered so that Wiley's former boss needed an airplane again. He ordered an improved model of the Vega from Lockheed and asked Post to come back to Oklahoma as the company pilot.

The newest Vega — also named *Winnie Mae* — was more powerful than the original, and Post wanted to see what it could do. The 1930 National Air Races offered the perfect opportunity — a prize for the fastest time between Los Angeles and Chicago — and the *Winnie Mae*'s owner agreed to let Post enter the airplane in the race. Wiley had plans to do more, however, than simply fly from California to Chicago faster than anyone else; he intended to continue to New York and set a new coast-to-coast speed record.

The Vega was a fast airplane, but some changes were needed for a trip that long. Post installed extra fuel tanks in the big cabin so he could fly farther without

Wiley Post received his sporting aviation license in 1930 from the National Aeronautic Association, the American branch of Federation Aeronautique Internationale. Orville Wright was president of the U.S. association, and his signature can be seen on the document.

refueling, and he modified the engine with a special supercharger so that it would perform better at high altitudes.

The supercharger was added because the *Winnie Mae*'s engine (like all aircraft engines except rockets) was an "air-breather," meaning it produced power by burning a combination of fuel vapor and air. The amount of power produced by the engine was therefore determined by the amount of air available. Because the air gets thinner with altitude, the engine would produce less and less power as the airplane climbed.

A supercharger ("super" for more than normal, "charge" for the supply of air), however, solves the problem. It is nothing more than a pump that supplies enough additional air to offset the power loss that normally occurs during a climb. With a supercharger installed, an engine can produce as much power at high altitude as at sea level, and the airplane can fly at much higher speeds. Flying higher also meant that Post could take advantage of the upper-level winds that blew across the United States from west to east, increasing his speed across the ground even more.

With extra fuel in the cabin tanks and the promise of flying higher and faster than anyone else, Post was all set for the race from Los Angeles to Chicago, and if all went well, to continue on to New York for a new transcontinental speed record.

Unfortunately, all didn't go well. Shortly after take-off, Post was led astray by a problem with the magnetic compass, and he spent forty minutes getting back on course. Post nevertheless managed to stay ahead of the other racers, and the *Winnie Mae* roared across the finish line in first place. The 1,760-mile (2,832-km) trip from Los Angeles had taken nine hours and nine minutes, fast enough to win the $7,500 prize and set a new record. The time lost to the compass problem, however, meant that a coast-to-coast record flight was out of the question.

Around the World in Record Time

By now, Wiley Post was convinced that the Lockheed Vega was the best airplane available for long-distance flights. As if the performance of the newer model weren't enough, the original *Winnie Mae* was also entered in the Los Angeles–Chicago race and finished in second place. Post was certain he could do more than set a new transcontinental speed record. He began to think seriously about flying around the world.

Both of the Vega pilots had chosen to get help with navigational details when they were planning the Los Angeles–Chicago trip. They turned to Harold Gatty, a graduate of the Royal Australian Naval College who operated a school for marine navigators and airplane pilots. His experience and knowledge would be invaluable to a pilot who was considering a long-distance flight. Post decided to call upon Gatty for not only the preflight planning, but to join him as navigator for the trip.

In 1931, Post (left) hired Harold Gatty (right) to be his navigator on their flight around the world.

Post now had three of the elements he needed: a fast and reliable airplane, a good navigator, and a desire to fly farther and faster than anyone else. He also felt that aviation needed something to get the public's attention, something that would stimulate passenger business. And so Wiley Post made a decision — he was going to fly all the way around the world in record time.

Harold Gatty was hired, and formal planning for the trip began in February 1931. There were many details to be considered in addition to selecting a route for the *Winnie Mae*. Gasoline and spare parts had to be stored at airfields along the way, permission to overfly each foreign country had to be obtained, weather conditions in remote parts of the world had to be studied. The list went on and on.

And there were more modifications to get the *Winnie Mae* ready for the trip. A larger fuel tank was installed in the cabin, blocking access to the cockpit. Post now had to enter and leave his "office" through a small overhead hatch. Gatty would be seated in a small compartment behind the tank, and a speaking tube was devised to link the two crew members. Engine noise made normal conversation impossible during flight. A hatch was cut in the top of the airplane so that Gatty could see the stars and use his celestial navigation equipment.

On May 23, 1931, the *Winnie Mae* arrived at Roosevelt Field, an airport just east of New York City. This was the same field from which Charles Lindbergh had departed for his solo transatlantic flight in 1927. Post and Gatty were well prepared and ready to go, but bad weather over the North Atlantic delayed departure for a full month.

They finally got into the air just before 5 A.M. on June 23. After more than a full day of flying and two refueling stops — one in Newfoundland, one in England — the *Winnie Mae* touched down at Templehof Airport in Berlin, Germany. Post and Gatty were scheduled for six hours of rest at this point in the trip, and they fell asleep with the knowledge that they had broken the transatlantic speed record.

The two aviators were airborne again early the next morning and headed for Moscow, the first of five stops in the Soviet Union. During the landing on Blagoveshchensk's rain-soaked runway, the *Winnie Mae* bogged down, and it took twelve hours to pull the airplane out of the mud. Post and Gatty got twelve hours of badly needed rest, but they also lost twelve hours in their attempt to break the record.

One more stop in Russia, then the *Winnie Mae* would fly 2,441 miles (3,928 km) over the Pacific Ocean to

(left) **Post is helped by local officials as he crawls out of the *Winnie Mae* after arriving in Berlin.** (above) **Post and Gatty chat with Berliners while mechanics service and repair the *Winnie Mae* during the brief stop in Germany.**

Alaska. Post guided the *Winnie Mae* through fog and rain for twelve hours and finally landed on a beach near Nome, Alaska, with the fuel tanks almost dry.

The takeoff from Nome was a near disaster. The Vega nosed over in the soft sand, and the propeller was badly bent. Post had to use all his skills as a mechanic; with a wrench, a hammer, and finally a rock, he was able to get the blades straightened enough to continue the trip to Fairbanks.

Post and Gatty were close to total exhaustion by this time, and they welcomed the chance to get several hours of sleep while mechanics replaced the damaged propeller. At 3:25 A.M. the next day, they were headed across the Canadian Rockies bound for Edmonton, Alberta, where they encountered yet another muddy runway. Post didn't want to take the chance of damaging the airplane on takeoff again, so telephone poles and wires were moved out of the way, the *Winnie Mae* was towed downtown, and Edmonton's paved main street became a runway.

The two aviators were soon flying over U.S. soil once again, and after a half-hour refueling stop in Cleveland, Ohio, they started the last leg of the trip. The *Winnie Mae* landed at Roosevelt Field at 8:47 P.M. on July 1, setting a new round-the-world record — eight days, fifteen hours, and fifty-one minutes.

Post and Gatty had traveled 15,474 miles (24,903 km) in eight and a half days, stopping for fuel and sleep fourteen times. The total flight time was 107 hours, the average airspeed was 146 miles (235 km) per hour, and the *Winnie Mae's* engine had run the entire time without missing a beat.

Near total exhaustion, Post and Gatty arrived at Roosevelt Field in New York City on July 1, 1931.

But equally astounding was Post's personal endurance. Throughout the entire eight and a half days (during which he had all the responsibility for the safety of the flight), he had slept only fifteen hours, never more than a few hours at a time. His ability to make good decisions in the face of extreme fatigue was remarkable, and would be even more essential for his next record-setting project: a flight around the world by himself.

(above) **Post and Gatty received lavish attention after their successful flight around the world. From left to right, Mrs. Gatty, Wiley Post, New York Mayor Jimmy Walker, Harold Gatty, and Mrs. Mae Post.**
(left) **Gatty and Post show off two of the many honors they received.**

Getting Ready for Another Record Flight

For several days after the record flight was completed, Wiley Post's life was a blur. Not only was he recovering from lack of sleep, but the parades, banquets, and celebrations in his honor took up much of his time. Post didn't think that he had achieved very much, but he was wrong. Much like Lindbergh's Atlantic crossing a few years earlier, the world-circling flight of the *Winnie Mae* called attention to the benefits of air transportation.

Post wanted to make the most of this publicity by touring the country in the record-breaking Vega, but the owner refused. The only solution was to buy the airplane, so Wiley scraped together $21,000 and purchased the *Winnie Mae*. With no one to answer to but himself, he could get on with the job of planning for his solo journey around the world.

One of the first things to be installed in the Vega was an automatic pilot, and Post tested it on a flight from Oklahoma City to Mexico City and back. With the autopilot to control the airplane while he napped, Post could cope with the fatigue that he knew would be his biggest single problem on the long solo flight.

He put more gas tanks in the cabin so that the *Winnie Mae* could fly even farther between fuel stops. But longer flights meant more fatigue, so he began a training program to prepare himself for long hours without sleep. For several weeks before the trip, he slept only in short naps and always at different times of day. He learned to relax totally and to keep his mind blank, letting his subconscious do all the thinking.

Pilots in the 1930s accepted accidents as part of the aviation business, but Post could not have anticipated the mishap that almost canceled his plans. He had invited another pilot to take up the *Winnie Mae* for a demonstration of the new autopilot, and almost immediately after takeoff, the engine quit and the Vega crashed into an orchard. It was later discovered that someone had stolen fuel from the airplane's tanks the night before.

Most of the *Winnie Mae* was shattered beyond repair, but with the help of a master woodworker, Post restored the airplane completely. In the process, he made some modifications that improved its performance even more. The fuel tanks in the wings were enlarged, and the entire passenger cabin was filled with tanks — the

Aviation manufacturers across the nation lent Post a hand by donating parts and services in his effort to fly solo around the world.

Four famous aviators gather to look at *Winnie Mae*'s radial engine. From left to right, Amelia Earhart, Wiley Post, Roscoe Turner, and Laura Ingalls.

Winnie Mae could now carry 645 gallons of gasoline. Post knew that as fuel was consumed during the flight, the center of gravity of the airplane would shift, so he installed a system of transfer pumps to help him maintain the proper balance in flight. A new type of propeller was installed; now Post could adjust the blade angle in flight to make the propeller more efficient.

When the "new" *Winnie Mae* was rolled out of the shop, it could lift more weight and fly faster and farther than before the accident. The performance was so much improved that Post changed his schedule to include only five refueling stops on his way around the world.

The cost of rebuilding the *Winnie Mae* left Post almost penniless, but a group of Oklahoma City businessmen donated enough money to keep the project going. The engine manufacturer furnished parts for the new power plant and sent one of their technicians to help prepare for the trip. The autopilot was provided free of charge by the manufacturer, who also sent a mechanic to help install it. One of the major oil companies agreed to provide fuel and lubricants all along the route. With solid financial support and the encouragement of the aviation community, Post went ahead with his plans.

The Lockheed Vega had become very popular in the 1930s, particularly among racing pilots. The speed and range of this streamlined airplane were responsible for a number of record-setting flights. Whenever a new record was set, someone went after it, usually in another Vega. Such was the case with Bennett Griffin and James Mattern, who in the summer of 1932 tried — unsuccessfully — to break the Post-Gatty round-the-world record.

In 1933, Mattern tried again, this time by himself, but his flight ended when engine trouble forced him down in a remote part of Siberia.

The First Solo Flight Around the World

By the end of May 1933, the *Winnie Mae* was ready to go. Post put the airplane through a final series of test flights and arrived at New York's Floyd Bennett Field in mid-June.

He intended to depart on July 1, but bad weather over the North Atlantic delayed the takeoff just like it had two years ago. There was no aviation weather reporting system in 1933. Pilots had to rely on observations from ships at sea, and the ships were seldom located along the route of flight.

Early in the morning of July 15, conditions over the ocean looked favorable, and Post lowered himself into the cockpit. At 5:10 A.M. the *Winnie Mae* lifted from the runway and almost immediately entered fog and clouds.

Post had become very good at flying "on instruments." When he couldn't see outside, he used the instruments on the panel in front of him to keep the *Winnie Mae* under control. In addition to the standard instruments that showed airspeed, altitude, and direction, he had installed an altitude indicator, a relatively new gyroscopic instrument with an artificial horizon that showed roll (wings banked, or inclined, left or right) and pitch (nose up or down). The altitude indicator also provided signals to the autopilot, which then operated the flight controls through a hydraulic mechanism to keep the airplane on course and at the desired altitude.

Wiley Post poses with two visiting French aviators, Maurice Rossi (left) and Paul Codos (right), nine days before his historic solo flight.

As soon as the *Winnie Mae* entered the clouds after takeoff from New York, Post engaged the autopilot and let it do the flying. It would take him one full day to cross the Atlantic and reach Germany, and he needed all the rest he could get.

Almost twenty-six hours after takeoff, the *Winnie Mae* touched down at Templehof Airport. Post had flown 3,942 miles (6,344 km), the first time anyone had flown nonstop between New York and Berlin.

The Germans had food and drink waiting for him, but Post refused. He had discovered that he was able to stay awake and alert longer if he went without food. "I don't want to eat," he said, "I don't want to shave, I don't want to bathe. I just want to clear out of here.

I flew here on tomato juice and chewing gum, and that's enough for me."

Just two hours and fifteen minutes later, Post took off for his second stop, the Russian town of Novosibirsk. Before he had gone very far, he discovered that the maps for his flight over Russia were missing, so he turned back and landed in East Prussia.

On top of that, a problem had developed in the autopilot. Post would have to fly the rest of the way by hand if he couldn't get it fixed. And as if that weren't enough, the weather ahead of him had gotten much worse. He gave up for the night and got six hours of badly needed sleep.

Next morning Post had a difficult choice to make. He could stop in Moscow and get the autopilot repaired, or he could continue, flying the *Winnie Mae* by hand and hoping he could stay awake. Then he remembered how badly he had been affected by fatigue on the first flight, and wisely decided to get the autopilot fixed.

Two hours and fifteen minutes after he landed in Moscow, Post was back in the air with a working autopilot. He reached Novosibirsk in thirteen hours and fifteen minutes. The missing maps were replaced, Post slept while the *Winnie Mae* was refueled, and in two hours he was on his way again.

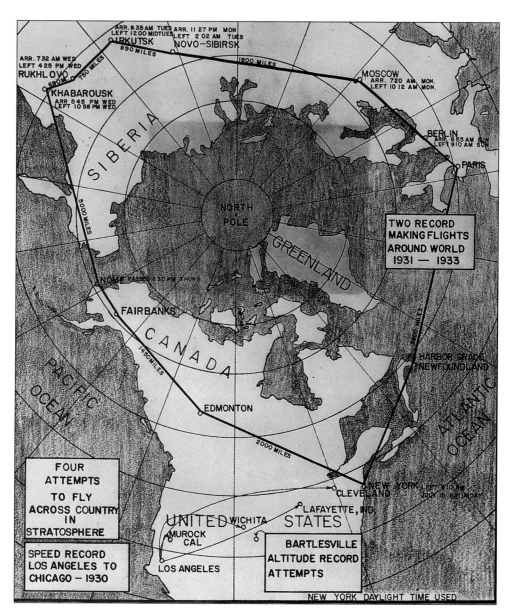

This map, drawn from a North Pole pespective, traces the route
flown by Post on his solo journey around the globe.

More trouble with the autopilot forced him to make an unscheduled stop at Irkutsk, Russia. There were reports of heavy thunderstorms over the mountains along the route, so Wiley elected to delay a few hours, giving him time to rest and giving the mechanics time to work on the autopilot.

Post had planned to follow the Trans-Siberian Railroad on this leg of the trip. Shortly after takeoff, however, the tracks disappeared into the rain and darkness, and the *Winnie Mae* wandered off course. After seven and a half hours in the air, Post spotted the town of Skovorodino and landed. He figured that he was slipping behind schedule, so he spent only a few hours on the ground, then took off for Khabarovsk, arriving there four and a half hours later.

There was no sleep for Post during this stop. He spent two hours studying weather maps for the next leg of the trip, a 3,100-mile (22,531 km) overwater flight to Fairbanks, Alaska, and the weather did not look good. After takeoff from Khabarovsk, he was forced to fly on instruments for seven straight hours, using the autopilot most of the time. He finally broke out of the clouds after climbing to 14,000 feet (4,828 km) above the sea.

When the mountains of Alaska's Seward Peninsula

came into view, Post brought the *Winnie Mae* down to 3,000 feet, followed the coastline to Nome, then headed east toward Fairbanks. But the combination of extreme fatigue, radio problems, and unfamiliarity with the Alaskan terrain soon had him completely confused. When he identified the tiny mining village of Flat, Alaska, he knew he was in no shape to continue the flight without rest and decided to land.

This was no big-city airport. The landing strip at Flat was only 700-feet (1,127-km) long, and there was a ditch running across the end. Post did the best job he could, but the *Winnie Mae* ran into the ditch, the right landing gear gave way, and the propeller was badly bent. He was safely on the ground, but once again Wiley Post was stopped short of his goal with a damaged airplane.

A group of miners went to work on the broken right wheel, and a pilot in Fairbanks volunteered to fly a mechanic and a new propeller to Flat. Post slept while the repairs were made, and the *Winnie Mae* was ready to go at dawn the next day. He flew to Fairbanks and refueled the airplane, then had to wait eight hours for favorable weather over the Canadian Rockies. He finally arrived at Edmonton after a nine-hour flight, much of it on instruments, and some of it at 20,000 feet (32,187 km) to avoid thunderstorms over the mountains.

Post now faced the last leg of the flight, and he was almost numb with fatigue. He had been flying the *Winnie Mae* most of the time for almost a full week. He knew that it would be impossible to stay awake the entire time between Edmonton and New York, so he fig-

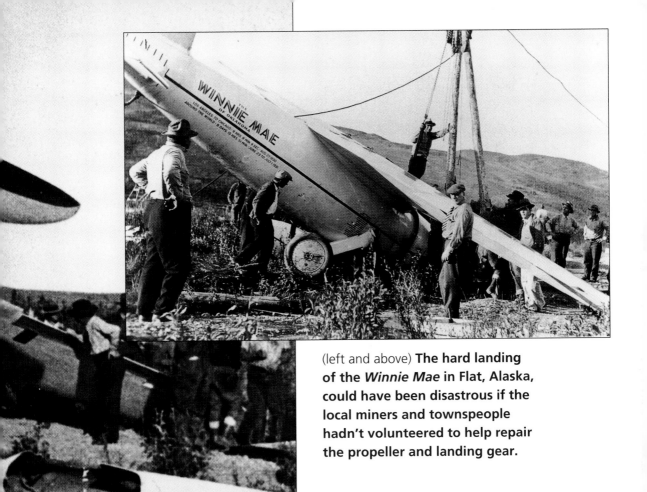

(left and above) **The hard landing of the *Winnie Mae* in Flat, Alaska, could have been disastrous if the local miners and townspeople hadn't volunteered to help repair the propeller and landing gear.**

ured out a way to keep from falling sound asleep. He tied a wrench to one of his fingers and held the wrench in one hand; when he dozed off and his grip relaxed, the wrench dropped, jerking his finger and waking him up.

The autopilot (which Post had named "Mechanical Mike") did most of the work while the *Winnie Mae* sped eastward across Canada and the northern United States. As he got closer to New York, his progress was reported by radio stations all over the country. Wiley Post was going to be a hero again.

It was late in the evening of July 22 when the *Winnie Mae* landed at Floyd Bennett Field, and Post was welcomed home by fifty thousand exuberant New Yorkers. The official time for the flight was seven days, eighteen hours, forty-nine and a half minutes, of which more than one hundred and fifteen hours were in the air. Wiley Post had broken his own previous record by more than twenty-one hours, became the first person to fly around the world twice, and the first person to fly around the world alone.

The Lockheed Vega deserved much of the credit for the new records and the advances in aviation technology that followed, but Post's determination and his skill as an aviator played an even larger part. Howard Hughes, another well-known pilot who broke the *Winnie Mae*'s record five years later, said "Post's flight was the most impossible bit of flying ever accomplished. As far as I'm concerned, his flight was the greatest of all time."

Fifty thousand New Yorkers greeted Wiley Post after his triumphant solo flight.

Thousands of New Yorkers lined
Broadway, blowing steamboat
whistles, streaming ticker tape,
and dropping paper. Wiley Post
made his way from the southern
tip of Manhattan toward City Hall
to receive an official decoration
from the mayor.

Wiley Post became an aviation researcher after the 1933 flight. His greatest enemy on both flights around the world had been bad weather. After months of trial-and-error tests, he created the world's first successful high-altitude pressure suit and developed air-  plane modifications that allowed extended high-altitude flights. At this time, Post alone seriously considered the possibilities of extended high-altitude airplane travel. By mid-June 1935, Post had spent more hours in the stratosphere than any other man and had traveled in the "jet stream" at sustained ground speeds of 300 miles (483 km) per hour for long periods.

Unfortunately, Post didn't live to see his research put to use. Post made his last flight on August 15, 1935, with his good friend Will Rogers, the famed cowboy humorist, as a passenger. The two were making an aerial tour of Alaska, when their plane crashed on takeoff from a small Inuit village near Point Barrow. Both were killed instantly.

(bottom) **Post and Rogers posed for photographers in Fairbanks, Alaska.** (middle) **Post and Rogers died instantly after their plane rose from the ground and plummeted in the muddy river lagoon, 15 miles from Point Barrow.** (top left) **Newspapers around the world announced the tragic news of deaths of aviator Wiley Post and humorist and columnist Will Rogers.**

The *Winnie Mae* is a permanent exhibit in the Smithsonian Institution's National Air and Space Museum in Washington, D.C., a symbol of those golden years in American aviation and a monument to Wiley Post and his achievements.

Facts, Figures, Important Dates

The Pilot — Wiley Hardeman Post

    Born — March 16, 1900; Grand Plain, Texas

    Dies — August 15, 1935; Point Barrow, Alaska

The Airplane — Lockheed Vega, the *Winnie Mae* (named for the daughter of one of the original owners)

    The Lockheed Vega was a single-engine, single-pilot monoplane. Molded spruce plywood was used in its construction; the resulting smooth curved surfaces made it a fast and efficient airplane. The Vega became one of the most popular models of its time.

Specifications:

    Length — 27 feet, 6 inches (8.38 m)

    Wingspan — 41 feet (12.49 m)

    Normal Weight — 2,918 pounds (1,330 kg)

    Weight fully loaded for long-distance trips — 3,200 pounds 1,370 kg)

Power Plant — Pratt & Whitney Wasp seven-cylinder radial air-cooled engine, 420 horsepower.

Statistics of the First Solo Flight Around the World:

Departed Floyd Bennett Field (New York City) on July 15, 1933.

Returned to Floyd Bennett Field on July 22, 1933.

Total elapsed time: 186 hours, 49.5 minutes

Total flight time: 115 hours, 36.5 minutes

For Further Reading

Berliner, Don. *Distance Flights.* Minneapolis: Lerner Publications, 1990.

Hayman, LeRoy. *Aces, Heroes, and Daredevils of the Air.* New York: Julian Messner, 1981.

Jeffris, David. *The First Flyers: Pioneers of Aviation.* New York: Franklin Watts, 1988.

Nevin, David. *The Pathfinders: The Epic of Flight.* Alexandria, VA: Time-Life Books, 1980.

Rosen, Mike. *The First Transatlantic Flight.* New York: Franklin Watts, 1989.

Taylor, Richard L. *The First Flight: The Story of the Wright Brothers.* New York: Franklin Watts, 1990.

Zisfein, Melvin B. *Flight: A Panorama of Aviation.* New York: Knopf, 1981.

Index

About the Author

Richard L. Taylor is an Associate Professor Emeritus in the Department of Aviation at the Ohio State University, having retired in 1988 after twenty-two years as an aviation educator. At retirement, he was the Director of Flight Operations and Training, with responsibility for all flight training and university air transportation. He holds two degrees from the Ohio State University: B.S. in Agriculture and M.A. in Journalism.

His first aviation book, *Instrument Flying,* was published in 1972, and continues in its third edition as one of the best-sellers in popular aviation literature. Since then, he has written five more books for pilots, and hundreds of articles and columns for aviation magazines.

Taylor began his aviation career in 1955 when he entered U.S. Air Force pilot training, and after four years on active duty continued his military activity as a reservist until retirement as a Major and Command Pilot in 1979.

Still active as a pilot and accident investigator in addition to his writing, Taylor flies frequently for business and pleasure. He and his wife live in Dublin, a suburb of Columbus, Ohio.